AN ECHO OF RE

by

GW00862648

Keith Ratcliffe

Typeset and Published
by
The National Poetry Foundation
(Reg Charity No 283032)
27 Mill Road
Fareham
Hants PO16 0TH
(Tel: 0329 822218)

Printed by
Meon Valley Printers
Bishops Waltham (0489 895460)

Sponsored by Rosemary Arthur

Cover Photograph by Celia Rambaut

Poems in this collection have previously been published in Outposts, Acumen, Doors and Envoi, and accepted for publication by *The Countryman*.

ISBN 1 870556 66 6

£4.50

CONTENTS

* * *

It is easy to dedicate these poems. My wife thought they should be seen as a token of the love I have for our two sons, Matthew and Peter, but, though she is right about the love I feel for them, I have no hesitation in dedicating this collection to the two whose constant efforts have made it possible –

For Vivienne

and

Peggy Poole.

Very few of us are given the privilege of facing our own death – not the 'some–un–numbered–day–in–the–future' of it; but the immediacy of 'today' or 'tomorrow' – the experience crystalizes the clarity of the important. If a Black Hole is an unimaginably intense density *of* matter, then the awareness of one's own impending death intensely densifies *what* matters. In some of the poems in this collection you are given an insight into that process, and are, in turn, privileged to be so.

Johnathon Clifford – Founder NPF

FOR ALEC

Significance seems often retrospective
and then elusive, too;
it's thirty years since I gazed and gazed
at beads of condensation glistening
on the hairy leaves of sundews
growing in the dankness of the rocks
of Harper Fell's east face,
and yet their gleam returned to mind
the night, three years ago,
when you and I looked up and saw
a meteorite burn brightly out.
You know we may be the only two
who witnessed that; it could be
that we gave the moment meaning, or
perhaps, it gave meaning to us.

We may surmise, but cannot know
its provenance, its origin;
we only really know its traverse must have been
between a million miles and a million years
unknown and maybe pointless till
that final fatal flash.
After its long, lonely journey
we saw its shining moment and now
I write and it survives
suspended in the space within my mind;
one of us is justified.

In "Sei carattere in cerca di un autore"
it's only when we hear aloud the scream
in its dénoument, we realise
the silent scream preceding it.
So with the gestation of a drop of dew,
so with the journey of a shooting star
so is it with my words that go unheard.

FLOWERS

It is hot in here
it is dry
a giant lithops
might easily be grown.
"Grau," Rilke wrote, "wie ein Markstein"
and this might be a nameless kingdom, too.
A kingdom peopled by dead souls
whom I have vaguely known;
the flowers from their funerals
are often sent, a gift
to cheer us patients...
They do not make me laugh;
a jar of maggots might.

I watch the plants die slowly...
a Kalenchoë lived two weeks
before it shrivelled up,
but that's a succulent;
cut flowers do not do so well,
no-one brings them water.
Their beauty lasts a day
or maybe two and they succumb,
drying, drooping, dropping, dying.
No, they do not cheer me up.

QUESTIONS: FOR MOLLIE

When people thought that I might die
I lay aware of all, or almost all.
Each word I heard with such a clarity
it was as if the voices had been tuned.
And yet it is not voices that I hear
when summoning that night:
it is a picture that I see, its theme
is angst with faces Dürer–drawn,
its focal point (I've never really understood)
a pair of hands grasped round
a vacuum flask...

Two questions, Mollie.
What was in the flask
and did you ever drink from it?

DUTCH ELM

The wind has gone like Shelley's
an enchantress gone
and it's not alone;
my thoughts are dead or dying
but each day peels away
another piece of bark,
each day brings another failure
and I find there's something else
I cannot do
and death's a little nearer.

It's rather like Dutch Elm disease:
when first it struck
I did not really notice:
just a leaf here, there
a branch.
Then suddenly it was obvious:
a tree here, there
a copse, and
one day all were gone.

There is a wickerwork or basketry container
on the television in the t.v. room.
It looks empty now but contains
a dead flower's remains.
I knew the plant quite well;
its fragile white petals
festooned around the basket's looped handle,
survived the heat a fortnight without water
or almost waterless.
One patient tended it, binding
etiolated growth round the handle's loop
watering it a little in a near perfunctory way.

He must have realised it would soon
join the bleak array of dead.
It may have been a gift for one already dead,
might have cheered him up.
But more likely it cheered, to some extent
relieved the frustration of, the one
who brought it here and now, nearly empty,
it stands in desiccated memory
of Gogol's book 'Dead Souls.'

THE DIFFERENCE

I've seen a lot of people die in here.
There are two types:
those the doctors fight to save
who die in a flurry of activity
that they must feel in vain;
the others simply fade
in virtual solitude and die.

Doctors at the start, see
in the first potential of success.
That final silence seems
an aftermath of failure.
The second kind
is a failure from the start.
Doctors know and nurses know,
and probably the patients know.

I am of the second kind:
each day I get a little,
almost imperceptibly, worse.
Doctors rarely visit me
or, if they do, it's only cursorily
that they pass by.
But I don't mind: they only speak
inanities and loudly, too.

Better that the elm
outlive the elm bark beetle.

A COLLISION OF KALEIDOSCOPES
(*For Ann*)

My mind sings on inside my silent shell
a synaesthetic kaleidoscope of random memories
poems and places, people, faces – all revolve;
I hear them all, I see them too.

It's near three hundred days now
that I've wasted in this ward.
I do not know how many patients I have seen
nor how many nurses, but
I have empathetic moments that recur,
enliven the kaleidoscope...

We shared such a moment, Ann;
no words, no need for words
just understanding laughter,
a collision of kaleidoscopes
an intermeshing of gears
when together we realised
what a myopic patient had been perusing,
through a reading glass, for some three days...

What letter has he reached
in that telephone directory?

URN

Someone who had heard or read my words
has moved the soil and pot, with its shrunken plant,
from the container, but it still stands empty
on the television in the t.v. room.

I look at it and see extended metaphors
but it does not look like my wheelchair
and the pot's not like my skull, not like my mind.
The soil won't have worms in it – too dry.
There might be microscopic insects
or rather, might *have* been.
Fungi are more likely to have taken root
but even they are gone.

Metaphors for ashes have been jettisoned
yet I remember when that container held a plant.
I look more closely at it now than any
mundane programme on the screen below.
I may appear a fool behind my silence's wall
but that apparent emptiness has memories for me
as I may have for it.

OWL

The Hegelian owl laps up the darkness,
unseen by human eye, or mostly so.
But every perch is marked
each intervening kill recorded
in the black bowl's infinitude.

Life goes on like that;
I used to think we left behind
a wake that ever is and ever dying
but in the night, the universe seemed vast
when as a youth I lay supine
on Carrock Fell in Cumberland
and gazed in awe at Leonid meteor showers,
perhaps naively wondering at the free display,
what seemed vast, seems little now.

Two million times the solar mass,
the last black hole they found;
more than enough, the silicon in that,
to code the history
of every human being that ever lived.

METEORITES

I saw Aida the first time in Rome
at the baths of Caracalla,
but it's not the opera I recall:
it is the lighting of the black sky
by a shower of meteorites.
It must have been July,
they, Leonids.

I never shall forget
the tumult of applause that followed
not each aria, but every flashing
shooting star. I wonder now
how many the theatre might hold:
how many still recall?

ANNA MARIA

Years ago I met a woman whom I loved,
not in a sexual way,
and have loved ever since.
I know, Anna Maria, that
you thought a lot of me
but you said *"non scivermi non risponderó."*
Do not write, I won't reply.

I stood forlorn,
stranded by the flood
on Florence Station
– it seems like yesterday –
yet now you must be old and might be dead:
I see now why you told me
not to write to you, and still I won't
but you'll not die while I'm alive
and I will write *of* you.

In the great bowl we both shall be
like shooting stars, like Hegel's owl:
permanent in our evanescence.
We may yet meet.

COMMUNICATION

If I could leap my silent wall
then so, of course, I would,
but it might only be to find
a further barrier, this time of words.

There may be those who understand
why I think of Keble before Herbert
when I look through a window:
"A man that looks on glass,
on it may stay his eye
or, if he pleaséth, through it pass
and then the truth espy."

There will be those who know
why I think of the college too,
maybe of both. But words are
clothing pegs: individual concepts grow
until they are too heavy for the peg
and fail, and failing, fall.
Emerging concepts are best shared in memory.

Who realises what I see in stones?
Who knows why I laugh at telephone directories?

FUCHSIAS

I used to grow fuchsias
and soon had an ambition
to grow standards – which I did
– but unknown to my sleeping wife, I spent
many an early morning hour looking,
simply looking, at the growing blooms.

I thought of Baudelaire's
"*les parfums, les couleurs*"
and "*les sons se répondent*,"
and wondered if the swelling buds
would slowly come to flower
or if, with a visual sound,
they'd burst into full bloom.

I do not know the answer yet –
I always fell asleep.

BY BEDSIDES

I'm glad that no-one brings me flowers:
the blossoms don't last long in here;
often their recipients last less.
They stay by bedsides, parching symbols
of their bearers' wordlessness.

One man has a cactus
and I think of that a lot;
but I do not think its owner does:
he may outlive it or it may outlive him;
it's certain to outlive all other plants in here.

CONSUMMATION

I cannot say with Ungaretti,
"I'm aglow with immensity."
I lighten my darkness
with a deeper dark, not light –
the dark has too much mass for that,
it pulls light back –
and if my lightness is darkness
(darkness after light,
the flash, for instance, of a meteorite)
then may you also know
that in my silence is the constant sound
of words you cannot hear, but words
I think, and thinking, often want
to say.
Darkness/light...silence/sound.
If only I could make my illness...health.

MORE FLOWERS

For three days, maybe four,
I watched a new arrival.
In that time he lay
prostrate,   motionless
save possibly some movement of the mouth.
People came to visit but
I do not think he knew,
despite that some stayed there all day.
Doctors came once, but not again.

On the first day he was brought
a bunch of flowers
red, pink, orange and yellow.
He did not see them.
Just as well – they died!
A second, more elaborate bunch
placed at the other end of the bed
fared better. It comprised
chrysanthemums,   carnations,   lilies,
and what looked from here
like a Sweet William. I'll never know:
he died, they disappeared.

The dead flowers still remain.

CANDLELIGHT

I've seen a thousand candles burning
in St. Albans' Abbey,
constant in their flicker, they
reflected the night sky, or seemed to.
But I could neither see nor hear,
only imagine, the whisper of its flight amongst the flames
of Hegel's fleeting symbol, owl.

But now I know that in the midst
of all those candles' light
no owl could have flown.
Perhaps the flicker symbol of the candlelight sufficed,
more lasting, more enduring even,
than the meteorites I love.

TRANSLATE, THEY NEED TO LISTEN

No moment is so difficult to bear
as when incompetents transfer me to the chair;
it's true they do not understand its ways
for they are not mechanics;
it's true they do not know my cushion makes me slip
unless I'm placed on it nearly directly.
But what upsets me most is when,
after my failure to obey their order: "**Bend!**"
they say, "Now don't be difficult, do not be awkward,
not so stiff or we'll put you back to bed."

They do not hear my silent words
that turn through screams to curses.
It may be just as well they don't:
I swear, especially in French.
Perhaps they'd think me mad,
or might they hesitate, and listen?

MATTHEW AND PETER

Another bunch of flowers is dying;
its vase will shortly join the bowl
to stand in emptiness.
The shooting star is now no more
than a memory of space and of Aida;
the owl has gone, leaving
just a feeling of its having been.
Yet I live on, and they
live on in me.
But am I recorded, will I
live on like that feeling of flight?
Or can I only hope that you,
my sons, remember me?

VÉROLE DE MOINE

At a school in Rennes
long years ago
a teacher called
Lemarchand or Lemannier
won *Le Grand Prix Catholique*
pour la Littérature
for his book "*Côté d'Ombre*."
His pseudonym was Sullivain.
I don't remember much of him
and he would not remember me.
But he did teach me
the title of a poem.

He did not mean to;
he never knew that I was there
when, in his priestly robes,
he passed me on the stair.
He tripped and swore but I still
remember these two things:
firstly that he was a teacher/priest;
secondly what he said:
the title of this poem.

"The last shall be first."
I'd often heard but rarely thought.
I used to run and even won
some very minor races,
but I was never really good.
I'd swim but never win
though once I came in last.
In most pursuits people
thought me better than I was
and often I would think so too.

I loved, still love, the Fells.
It's no surprise, in view
of all the time I'd spend in hills,
that I should become known
as something of a mountaineer,
but what I always tried to hide
was the fear that seized me
on the cliffs, in storms, or even
watching friends stand near a drop:

but now I stand a better chance
of coming first by being last
and I do not mean I cannot walk.
I fly within my mind from place to place
at speeds inconceivable in any race;
one blink of my eyes gives time
to hear a symphony and, inside,
my silence comes aloud to life.

MUSHROOMS

I liked to teach my sons about the world;
I taught myself much of the time
though often in vanity I would pretend
to know already what I was showing them.
My pride at Matthew's ability to identify
unerringly between *agaricus campestris*,
arvensis, and the *amanitas* was both in his
precociousness but, albeit in my ignorance, vicarious.

I shall not forget the day he told me
in excitement, he had found *agaricus campestris*
growing "just around the corner" from our St. Albans home.
"Come on I'll show you, Dad" was his response to disbelief.
They were growing on the surface of a grave
in the cemetery nearby, round and plump,
their whiteness luminescent in the graveyard shade.
I picked some, but did not take them home to eat.

There were small holes in the gills.
Perhaps they had been made by maggots,
maggots who came, perhaps, from deeper down.

BLACKBIRD

It's four days since last the blackbird sang;
the young by now are fledged and flown
not just the nest but also territory.
The hole of silence, where its song
once warned all others, reminds me
of our growing boys:

one, aggressive, violent
towards my illness and, unintentionally,
its container – me;
the other, in his absence, grieving
silently the man I used to be.

THESSALONIAN OWL

The thief that comes by night
might be an owl in search of prey
its furtive swoop unheard,
though not unsensed,
between the graves,
as testify the pellet coffins
of regurgitated bones
that lie scattered above
the more orderly rows of human bones
that rot in the uneaten flesh
...beneath.

BATS

There cannot be much time left to me now;
my wife has touched our elder son with fear
that death awaits me when I go to Austria
in two days time, but I've no fear of death
not when, nor where;
to compare a life-time with eternity
makes years quite pointless,
days so insignificant.

The 'how' might matter
but it would not be for long,
not even in a life-time:
the echo, maybe,
of the echo-sounder of a bat.

THE RAT-HOLE

In Dove's Nest crag
up in Combe Ghyll
the cliff has slipped.
It is possible to wriggle like a maggot
deep within the mountain side
and chew in the anatomy of earth.

Deep inside the graveyard
maggots do not have to stop and take their lunch
nor thrust and struggle to overcome
a barrier round essential nothingness:
they simply chew and, having chewed, dilate.
What they eat may live or die;
they do not, cannot know
but oh! the flowers above
are cared for with unconscious paradox.

Was it fear of silence
that made my friends and me shout in the dark
with silly jokes each time we climbed
the so-called Rat-Hole in Dove's Nest?
Or was it fear of death?

BLACKBIRD'S RETURN

They did not think that I'd return
from my last bout of illness.
It seemed, that thief by night,
would shortly sneak on board.

But death did not call
and like the blackbird singing
I came back at dawn.

LEAD MINE

As a boy I was intrigued to read
on the one inch Ordnance Survey
'Old Lead Mine.' The map
led me soon to Bannerdale
where fifty yards into the gloomy shaft
its barrel roof was lined with quartz,
quartz heavy with galena.

Why was it that whoever mined
the dankly hidden vein
could daily clamber such a way
yet leave so much behind?

CAVES

Deep in mine-shafts, pot-holes, caves,
I've often closed my eyes,
turned off my lamp
and known what total darkness is.
But in that black was always sound: the drip
of water from the tip of stalactite
to splash in pools below
or the dank noise of melting
in Grisedale's disused mine.

Yet even that sound was unique:
clear and hollow, almost metallic,
tempo and resonance always peculiar.

Is this how Mendelssohn heard each note
when he was on Iona?

PIERS GHYLL

Whitewater Dash, Grains,
Tilberthwaite and Sourmilk Ghylls,
Scales Force, Lodore Cascade and
Sailhow Beck are more than merely names
of lakeland streams and waterfalls to me.

I see and hear them all;
they mark paths to fells I've climbed.
I've sat and eaten by them,
even climbed within their beds,
some in frozen winter silence, too;
but never have I climbed, nor sat beside,
the jagged chasm of Piers Ghyll.

A path to Sca Fell crosses near it
and men have fallen to be lost and die
to the sound–defying silence
of its sepulchral depths.

GABBRO

Gabbro and Granophyre
the acrid climbers' rocks that line
the eastern face of Carrock Fell;
Gabbro, the leg-tearing
boulders to the south.
The Romans had a gold mine there
but, though I searched, I never found
the smallest piece of ore.

But an ore, more dense than gold,
glistens in my mind
of memories of the hill fort
in gaunt rings around the top,
the burial mounds beneath
and showers of shooting stars.

IN MEMORY OF FOSCOLO

I thought the Nigerian
in the bed facing mine
had died, but
he was only dying.

Were I a stone mason
I would prepare an Anglo-Saxon cross
of Black Cuillin gabbro
and make a plinth of porphyry
from Buchaille Etive Mor:

its redness would commemorate
the redness of his mouth;
I'd cap the whole with polished tiger stone,
with agate chisel an inscription on the plinth
and add "also in memory of Foscolo."

THE CLOVEN STONE

Round White Horse Bent
beyond the Glenderamackin watershed
north of Blencathra's summit
on Skiddaw's forest
stands the Cloven Stone.

Hidden in so bleak a place
the name assumed a mystery to me.
Cumbria has many strange–shaped rocks
without a name. I often dwelt
upon the Cloven Stone, but in reality
it is a piece of rock
of no remarkability.

I can think of many rocks with obvious gashes
more deserving of the name
yet the image in my mind remains
potent in its overtones.

CEMETERY GATES

The man in the bed facing mine
had gone home, but not to Ghana.
I could not forget him,
not dismiss the cemeterial stones
that were his eyes.
The tomb-stones he looked blankly through
would glare a glazen stare
hypnotically at me
which seemed to tell me how he yearned
for Ghana, longed for home.

The doctor, in response to what
was to be a last request, said
he would have to fly and
"there might be some trouble
in arranging it."

The smile, that I gave myself, was wry.
The next day I saw him collapse and die.
He was in Ghana. He had found
the fastest way to fly.

Gabbro occurs in Carrock Fell in Cumbria
re-emerging in the Isle of Arran
where its jagged high point is Goat Fell;
but in the Black Guillins
it reaches its contorted height.
Sgurr Nan Cillean
is mountain elegance par excellence
but there are other, weirder peaks:
Sgurrs Mhic Coinnich and Am Bhasteir,
The Bhasteir Tooth and Inaccessible Pinnacle,
Clach Glas, like fangs arise,
like writhing, rotting dorsal fins
thrown up and cast
in the eruption of their birth.

GRAVEYARD

My graveyard theme is superficially similar
to Foscolo's in his work *'I sepolcri'*
but my cemetery's stones are in the shapes
of crags that I have climbed
or climbed beside:
Gillercombe and Bowfell Buttresses, the Needle,
Troutdale Pinnacle and Gimmer Crag
loom lakeland through the mist.

From Glen Coe's keeper
Buchaille Etive Mor,
in shades of bloodened porphyry
I see the Crowberry Tower emerge
and, lastly, from the Cuillins
the menace of the Bhasteir Tooth
the Executioner's Axe.

BIRDSONG REVIVED

The music of the silences
that lie between Messaien's notes
are resonant with memories
and electrically alive with evocations;

I recall the cry of golden plover
high above Axe Edge
but more than them it is the being there
that they recall.
And not just there.

It is the fleetingness impreigned with permanence;
closing my eyes, I see them too
and, on Ramshaw Rocks, a merlin
scans the moor for prey.

AFTERMATH

Between the interstices in sound
in networks, too, of space
moments seem endless like a sleep
or in an eye–blink like a dream,
a dream perhaps of death:

music often seems most poignant in its silence;
notes in memory are never sullied
and in the silence after sound recalled
there lies unblemished music:

sound without a note
against the background of a perfect picture,
a painting with no brushstroke
a poem without a word.

SPLINTER

A wooden splinter killed Cogidumnus
according to the Venerable Bede;
but it may have been a smaller thing
that killed the King.

Not even Bede could see a microbe, yet
the body might have held some millions.
We cannot see the myriad worms
that slide in an incessant silence
underneath the graveyard's seeming emptiness:
they maggot on even between the wing–beats
of omniscience.

Perhaps it is easiest to think
a splinter killed a King.

DIES IRAE

My prison does not have stone walls
no iron bars;
my prison is the silence that's perceived.

But in my mind I hear my requiem,
I feel my wrath, although
it's not my music I can hear.

The bleak percussion of old pans clanking
on the imprisoning wire of Dachau
is emptily insistent, drowning

the crescendos from Verdi and from Mozart
in my mind. My loss is only
that of sound, or being heard;

the loss of those whom Penderecki mourned
was greater than his own,
greater than any individual's could be.

In his *'Dies Irae'* the wrath is glacial:
a generation is remembered.
My loss is insignificant recalling that.

CURTAIN

The lightning that I saw strike Pillar Rock
flung wide the veiling clouds;
it and the curtains on the boat
where deep in darkness
I lay near to death
brought back two thoughts
which bore comfort, brought security.

I remembered what Paul wrote
about the light that shines through darkness
and heard again the hymnwright's words
"Thou still, small voice of calm."

DREADFUL INJUNCTION

I've known my wife for twenty-seven years
and in that time she's never said to me
those words that any poet hates to hear:
"write me a poem!"

Any poem that I write I write for her,
every time I touch a key;
I touch it with the hindsight of those years
remembering that gamut of emotions
we have shared.
She knows the exhortation would be futile,
prove fruitless: she is
after that time beginning
to get to know me. Does that mean
that some day perchance, I might know her?

BY CHERWELL'S BANK

The Isis seemed so powerful, so fast, so smooth,
when slicing through it in the power of an eight;
not like the Cherwell, swirling
in its dipping willows' shade.

You cannot know how pleased I was
at your recall of that day long ago
when by your silence you gave your assent.

Yet what I thought love then
was not what I know now and need.
How could I know how great
my need and love of you would be?
You could not know how great
that would become.

THUNDER

There was a storm last night
the same as any thunderstorm
except perhaps the stage effects
were overdone,
but one thing differed:

two infant visitors, overcome
by excitement, laughed
and shouted at the brash display
of light and sound.

Their father told them,
"stop it, please be quiet,
these people here are sick."

Inwardly I smiled;
outwardly all was vivid,
the thunder's crash almost continuous.
The children's shouting?
Quite inaudible.

CALMATI

When climbing crags
I often had, it seemed, to choose
between life and death.
The choice was always life
the difference a finger's grip,
a stretch.

What never changed
was the moment of cold fear
preceding the commitment
and, when committed, the feeling
that the movement gave
a kind of grace,
a moment when the evanescent
assumed fleeting permanence.

I thought it was a feeling
not to be had again
but I found it on the Channel
as I lay quite close to death.
There was a choice to make,

HELIX

A single day, thought Camus' Meursault,
in a prison cell
would be enough to give a life–time
of analysis and that's a thought
I've often had; it's only days remembered,
days recorded, that really count.

Old photographs and old accounts,
poems bring moments, incidents alive
and in their living I survive.
Memories reach like huge, translucent,
scientific models, towards the infinite
of one of Crick and Watson's helices;
all are linked except perhaps the first and last
and death alone will make that helix circular.

Like meteors the memories in silence
fly against the blackness of night sky;
photographs might curl, might fade,
but many thoughts and feelings,
not just mine, fight in magnetic grip
against that Carey – time.

THE SOUND OF SNOW

The kind of silence that holds Lakeland
after heavy snowfall
is textured by the ice–melt,
punctuated by its rhythmic drips
and vainly holding in a muffled tone
the noise of wrestling captive falls.

It lies, a cold sarcophagus
for autumn's bracken, provides
a desolately resonating background
for the raven's croak.

COLD FELL

I always thought snow
melted from the top
but it's not always so.
The ground need only be
a little warmer than the freezing air
when the snow fell.

I first became aware
snow could melt upside down
when standing on Cold Fell's summit
on what seemed a foot of it.
I saw a pygmy shrew pop up
and eat my sandwich crumbs.

So when, from Carlisle's Eden Bridge,
the Pennines look unbroken white
there might be shrews
within a hidden labyrinth
above the concealed heather's roots.
It might be melting upside down.

INCANDESCENCE
(On hearing of a proposed reduction in his physiotherapy)

The lights that through my illness's
darkness gleamed are fading
fading quickly now,
my arms and hands move less and less;
without the help of physio
there is no way I can move the pall.

The curtains now may close
and I will drift away
perhaps to the dark point of origin
of shooting stars.
How long seems our life
when compared with theirs,
how brief compared with rocks,
time   petrified
and how much briefer still
than that before eternity.

MINERVAN DAWN

"Like a jig–saw puzzle
this sky serene
with some great clipper
in a sunset bay
a childhood ending
to a childhood day."

So I wrote when young, but now
the dusk does not descend
with that same measured calm;
"Dubito," wrote Sartre, *"ergo sum"*
but when the dusk has sped away
and night like a Minervan shadow
has usurped the day
then I think dawn may not descend:

perhaps I'm on the wrong side
of day and night, darkness
might be receding light
stars the smallest and the greatest
points to see. Night
might be clearer than bright day
and light lie hidden there.
I know now why Damascus had to be.

FOUNDRY

I cannot change the theme of what I write
for as I worm into the earth
I do not know what words may lie ahead
nor what ores may glint
within the darkness of approaching death.
I only know that I must pluck
each point of light from what
could easily be gloom, hope its vein
leads to unbroken brightness.

In the foundry
white hot sheets of metal, waiting
to be rolled into steel tubes
(splashes spluttering around)
might almost lie beyond
the darkness of the underworld seen
by Rilke's blind man on the bridge.

ROCKCLIFFE MARSH

I still can hear
the melancholy piping of redshanks
wheeling around their nests
in tufts of grass grown taller, greener,
feeding on the nitrates
in the dung of cattle grazing there.

They not only grazed
but also died, trapped
in the quicksands of the saltmarsh creeks.
The piping was their only orison.

I have seen many certificates and diplomas,
many gilded trophies too
but only in my mind.

They're for Narinder Kaur
the nurse with elegant hands
and read embossed with truth:

"World record, established September 1990,
for wet–shaving, bathing (with hair–wash)
and application of gels to gums and teeth

27 minutes." Signed by me.
So fast were you there was no time for thanks,
so please
may I thank you now?

ON A THREATENED MOVE TO A GERIATRIC WARD

The silence you perceive in me
is full of sound, words I cannot speak
conversations that you cannot hear
but to put me in a geriatric ward
would put a stop to all that noise.

No grunt when what I want is *"Yes,"*
no cough or splutter when it's *"No!"*
My silence would be muffled by a silence more complete
like the silence that surrounds a drop about to drip
from the tip of a stalactite
down in the deepest cave.

FOR BARBARA

Rilke saw a blind man
at the centre of the universe;
Saul had to go blind
so that he could see;
I lost my speech
yet now speak through the written word.

My God, two million times the solar mass
the last black hole discovered
is thought to be!
How small, how insignificant
that makes us seem.
And yet we know that You see all
and, even in our silence,
You hear our every call.